The Active Life

Parker J. Palmer

Leader's Guide

HarperSanFrancisco
A Division of HarperCollins*Publishers*

Leader's Guide prepared by Kathy Yanni

FIRST EDITION

Library of Congress Cataloging-in-Publication Data for original title
Palmer, Parker J.
    The active life: a spirituality of work, creativity, and caring /
Parker J. Palmer.—1st. ed.
        p. cm.
    Includes bibliographical references.
    1. Spirituality. I. Title.
    BV4501.2.P313 1990   89–45932   248.8'8—dc20   CIP
    ISBN 0-06-066457-6

ISBN 0-06-066459-2 (Leader's Guide)

92 93 94 95 96 97 98 ❖ DICK 10 9 8 7 6 5 4 3 2 1

Contents

Introduction

"My aim in this book," writes Parker J. Palmer in *The Active Life*, "is to celebrate and criticize the active life, to explore its joys and pains, its problems and potentials, to understand the forces that both drive and deform our activity—but to do all this with reverence for the mystery of self-discovery and creation which is at the heart of human action" (p. 11). Through a creative exploration of the truths embodied in the imaginative patterns of stories and poems, Palmer mines the riches of diverse traditions—Taoism, Judaism, Christianity, the contemporary struggle for social justice—while probing the depths of his own experience. With penetrating insight, he guides us into a searching examination of the truth inside us and the truth around us. In the harmony between these two realities, we discover the exhilarating freedom for the active life.

Palmer paints a vision for becoming "fully alive"—a way of living that unites contemplation-and-action. This paradoxical tension brings the strength of self-knowledge to bear upon our relationships with other human beings, nature, and God. Learning right action teaches us to become more honest with ourselves while unveiling the truth of our interconnectedness in "the entire community of creation." Palmer's culminating vision is the horizon of new life, a resurrection into the great community of justice, truth, and love.

The Active Life challenges us to creative reflection and authentic action as we discover the deep points of connection between self, world, and spirit. In the context of group discussion, it provides opportunities for discovering the "gift of community" as we learn with each other how to become more aware, more active, more caring human beings.

Starting an Adult Study Group and Using This Leader's Guide

Harper's series of Leader's Guides provides resources for small adult study groups. Each Guide is based on a widely read book by a well-known and knowledgeable author. Each provides suggestions for forming small groups and for leading the discussions. The Guides also provide discussion questions and other material that can be photocopied for participants.

Harper's Leader's Guides are designed for use in Christian churches of all denominations. However, they may also be used in other settings: neighborhood study groups, camps, retreat centers, colleges and seminaries, or continuing education classes.

Format

Harper's Leader's Guides have been planned as a basis for six one-hour sessions. Six weeks of discussion allows for depth and personal sharing, yet it is a limited commitment, one that busy adults find easier to make.

The Leader's Guides can be adapted for use in other time frames. By combining sessions, you can discuss a book in four meetings. Or, by being very selective with questions, you can plan a single two-hour session. The Guides can also serve as the foundation for a weekend retreat: the six hour-long sessions are alternated with recreation, rest, meals, and other activities.

Forming a Group

Choose a book that you think will be of interest to people in your congregation or other setting. Use your parish newsletter, announcements in services, visits to existing groups, and word of mouth to inform potential participants of the upcoming opportunity. It may be helpful to plan a brief orientation meeting for interested people.

An effective discussion group can be formed with as few as three or four adults joined together by a common interest. If more than twelve people respond, they should probably be divided into smaller groups.

Participants should have access to the books at least a week before the first session. Books may be ordered through your local bookstore or from Customer Service, HarperSanFrancisco, 151 Union Street #401, San Francisco, CA 94111, or call toll-free: 800–328–5125. Plan ahead and allow about six weeks for delivery.

At the time they receive their books, participants should also receive the material found at the back of this Leader's Guide: Materials for Group Distribution. You may photocopy this section to hand out. You may want to distribute all of the materials initially or you may distribute the information one session at a time.

Ask participants to take time to look these over before the session. The prepared discussion questions will serve as a medium to share insights, clarify questions, and reinforce learning.

Helps for Leaders

1. Be clear in announcing the time and place of the first meeting. If possible, choose a pleasant, comfortable room in which to meet where chairs can be set in a circle. This usually encourages more discussion than a formal classroom setting does.

2. Choose a leadership style: one person may lead the discussion in all six sessions, or there may be two people who co-lead every session or who alternate sessions. Leadership may also be rotated among the participants.

3. The Leader's Guide contains several kinds of questions. Some focus on what the book says. Do not neglect these; they are basic to intelligent discussion. These are also good questions for drawing more reluctant members into the discussion. Other questions deal more with the meaning and implications

of the author's words. Still others ask participants to share experiences, ideas, and feelings of their own.

4. In the Leader's Guide you will find sample responses to questions. These are not to be considered the "right answers." They are only suggested responses, which often direct you to particular passages in the book. Be open to participants' responses that may stray from these suggested answers.

5. Materials for Group Distribution, found at the back of this Guide, can be photocopied for your group.

6. Don't feel that you have to "get through" all the questions and suggested activities in the Leader's Guide. Choose only those that seem most important to your group.

7. Try to avoid having one or two people monopolize the discussion. Call on some other participants to share their thoughts.

8. If the group spends too much time on one question, or if it goes off on a tangent, gently call it back to the topic by moving on to another question.

9. Encourage openness and trust in the group by being willing to share your own thoughts. Try to establish an atmosphere in which all ideas are treated with respect and seriousness.

10. The Leader's Guide contains some suggestions for group process. Experiment with these, and feel free to adapt them to your particular group.

Preparing for Session 1

If you have time, read through *The Active Life* before your group meets for its first session. Grasping the book as a whole will give you a deeper understanding of it as you move through each chapter with the group. After familiarizing yourself with the book, read through this Leader's Guide, noting the structure of your sessions and the kinds of questions you'll be reflecting on together.

Before session 1, read the first two chapters of *The Active Life* and work through the session 1 discussion questions on your own—without relying on the printed comments and suggested responses. You may find it helpful to use a separate notebook for your answers, comments, and questions.

At least a week before the first group session, distribute to each participant a copy of *The Active Life* and a photocopy of the discussion guide for session 1 at the back of this Leader's Guide. (You may want to hand out all the Materials for Group Distribution at this time.) Ask participants to read chapters 1 and 2 of *The Active Life* and answer the discussion questions for session 1 before the first meeting. Confirm time and location.

This Leader's Guide has been created as a resource to provide all you need for reflecting on *The Active Life* in a group study context. However, this doesn't mean that you and the group must accomplish or discuss everything it suggests. You may find that you don't have time for all the questions listed. Use your judgment, and the group's expressed preferences, to select those questions you want to focus on—perhaps at the opening of each session, as this Guide occasionally prompts you to do.

Remember to check the "Session Materials" list before each session and gather the needed supplies to bring with you. There are suggested activities for closing each session, including an alternative for groups who may not be comfortable with an overtly religious or Christian emphasis. Adapt these suggestions to your group as appropriate.

Session 1: The Paradox in Becoming Fully Alive

The Active Life, chapters 1 and 2

Session Objectives

- To understand how contemplation and action form a paradox necessary to the experience of being "fully alive"

- To explore the nature of contemplation and the nature of action as two key dimensions of spirituality and life

- To become aware of how this understanding of paradox can strengthen our individual sense of self and our place in the world

Session Materials

- Copies of *The Active Life* for newcomers

- Extra photocopies of the discussion guide for session 1

- A Bible for each participant, or for every two participants

- Chalkboard and chalk; or large poster paper and markers; or overhead projector and blank transparencies

- Photocopies of the discussion guide for session 2 for distribution to each group member

Opening

Welcome participants as they arrive, and make sure each has a copy of *The Active Life* and a photocopy of the discussion questions for session 1.

After all have arrived, introduce yourself and review the group's scheduled time and place for future sessions. Then ask the group to break into pairs, choosing another person they don't know very well. (If there's an uneven number of people, complete the remaining pair yourself.) Allow one minute per person for interviewing partners in preparation for introducing that partner to the group when you reassemble.

After each person introduces his or her partner, start your reflection time together.

Reflecting Together

1. What questions or reflections about your own life, if any, do Palmer's insights in these first two chapters stimulate for you? Briefly describe these questions or reflections—or why you don't have any yet.
Encourage many participants to share brief, general impressions of the book, without extending into lengthier responses that you will explore with the other questions in this session.

2. The following pair of statements is one way of representing the opposing tensions of the active life and the contemplative life:
"Don't just stand there—do something."
"Don't just do something—stand there."

In your experience, how are these statements reflected in society—including religious communities—today?
Examples include the performance emphasis in our achievement-oriented society; the assumption that busyness equals productivity, or is evidence of personal importance; understandings of spirituality that place contemplation nearer to God than action; religious emphases on personal piety without recognizing the need for service, or vice versa; and so on.

3. Palmer defines action as "any way that we can co-create reality with other beings and with the Spirit" (p. 17). According to this definition, what are some of the ways in which you live the active life?

Possible answers might include: work, vocation, relationships, art, sport, ministry—any "visible form of an invisible spirit" or "outward manifestation of an inward power" (p. 17).

4. Palmer defines contemplation as "any way that we can unveil the illusions that masquerade as reality and reveal the reality behind the masks" (p. 17). According to this definition, what are some of the ways in which you live the contemplative life?

Possible answers might include: time set apart for meditation, prayer, or solitude; the habit of reflecting on events in order to gain a deeper understanding of them; reading; working through internal issues, with others or alone; writing for meditation or therapy.

5. According to Palmer, we should "try to live responsively to both poles of the contemplative-active paradox. But we must honor the pole of our own calling, even as we stay open to the other, lest we lose our identity, our integrity, our well-being" (p. 7).

As a help for understanding the journey of your own soul, use the following chart to identify your personal tendencies along the continuum between action and contemplation. For each set of poles, check the box along the continuum that best represents you.

	Strongly dominant	Tends to dominate	Blend	Tends to dominate	Strongly dominant	
Action	☐	☐	☐	☐	☐	Contemplation
Do	☐	☐	☐	☐	☐	Think
Spontaneity	☐	☐	☐	☐	☐	Preparation
Outward	☐	☐	☐	☐	☐	Inward
Struggle	☐	☐	☐	☐	☐	Quietness
Interaction	☐	☐	☐	☐	☐	Solitude
Take risks	☐	☐	☐	☐	☐	Plan ahead
Act	☐	☐	☐	☐	☐	Analyze

Share the insights you gained about yourselves from this exercise. Consider breaking the group up into twos or threes to facilitate easy personal discussion. Ask the group to reflect on how their insights can help them understand what it means to live with paradox in the spiritual life.

6. An "instrumental" act is one taken in order to reach some predetermined end or result. An "expressive" act is one taken simply because it expresses one's inner gift or truth, without worry over "how things will turn out" (see pp. 23–24). What are some areas of your life in which an expressive understanding of action could encourage you to take risks by relieving anxiety over results or outcome?

If necessary, review Palmer's explanation of these two concepts and use his examples to get discussion going (p. 22)—self-expressive acts of creativity, such as writing; caring deeply for another person; joining a cause.

7. Contemplation takes place in spontaneous moments of insight as well as in structured techniques—". . . life makes contemplatives of all of us, whether we want to be contemplatives or not. The only question is whether we can name and claim those moments of opportunity for what they are" (p. 26). How would you advise an action-oriented person to recognize and learn from opportune moments of contemplation?

As an example, Palmer discusses disillusionment and pain (pp. 26–27) as evidence of contemplation at work to rid us of illusions.

8. In the paradox of "contemplation-in-action," both tensions are necessary. "When we abandon the creative tension between the two, . . . action flies off into frenzy . . . contemplation flies off into escapism" (p. 15). How can these opposing tensions work together to help us learn to "celebrate the gift of life"?

Invite participants to choose a tension and share their thoughts on how it can help moderate the opposite extreme.

9. **Palmer says that we have an inner voice that sometimes tells us, "We need to accept death . . . or we will spend our energies building houses of cards . . . [Death] will sweep all our works away" (p. 20). How do you respond to this voice? Do you agree with it? Why or why not?**

This is another case of paradoxical tension. To stimulate discussion, you might want to ask the group to reflect on how to avoid the extremes of playing it too safe versus pursuing foolish dreams.

10. **What makes the difference between action that is fueled by an inflated ego and action that contributes to the development of a healthy ego?**

Palmer suggests that action is necessary to the development of a healthy ego, that we can learn about ourselves and our gifts through action. But he also points to the risk we take by acting, the risk of acting in ways which are driven by an inflated ego, the risk of acting in ways that impose our own ego-designs on others.

11. **"Contemplation and action are not high skills or specialties for the virtuoso few. They are the warp and weft of human life, the interwoven threads that form the fabric of who we are and who we are becoming" (pp. 18–19). How can these two dimensions help you grow into a stronger sense of self and a better understanding of your place in the world?**

Answers here will vary according to individuals. Palmer's major emphasis is that action and contemplation work together to give us new insights about ourselves, which become the truth that we offer each other in community.

12. **The author's mountain-climbing story (pp. 32–33) illustrates the active life as risk. Have you ever had an experience in which you knew you had to go all the way through it—"ride the monsters all the way down" (p. 33)—because it defied all**

your efforts to control or manage it? If so, what did you learn from the experience?

Share experiences with each other, looking for ways that these personal stories reveal "'the hidden wholeness' that lies beneath the broken surface of our lives" (p. 29). You may want to pair off once again, with different partners this time, to share your answers.

Looking Ahead

After confirming the time and place of your next meeting, be sure that all participants have a copy of the discussion guide for session 2. Ask them to read chapter 3 and answer the questions before the meeting.

Consider inviting participants to keep a notebook or journal for the duration of the study. In addition to providing a place to write down their responses to discussion questions, it would create an opportunity to record their insights, questions, struggles, and hopes prompted by working through *The Active Life*. If they are inexperienced with journaling, suggest types of entries they could make, such as:

- Questions or comments arising from their reading

- Significant quotes from the book

- A list of reading resources mentioned in the book or in other sources

- Reflections on how Palmer's insights relate to their personal experience

- A record of how various daily experiences contributed to or got in the way of the goal of "aliveness"

- Significant experiences, questions, or reflections that come up during group sessions

Closing

Divide the group in half and rearrange seating accordingly, with each side facing the other. Read the following pairs of Scripture passages antiphonally, alternating from side to side.

First side:	*Second side:*
Psalm 46:10–11	James 1:22–25
Psalm 27:14	Psalm 83:1
Luke 17:20–21	Matthew 6:9–10
Ecclesiastes 2:17–20	Ecclesiastes 3:10–14

Alternate closing: Spend two minutes in quiet, personal reflection on the goal of being fully alive in the coming week.

Session 2: The Shadow Side of Action

The Active Life, chapter 3

Session Objectives

- To critique distorted versions of the active life
- To understand the nature of authentic action

Session Materials

- Copies of *The Active Life* for newcomers
- Extra photocopies of the discussion guide for session 2
- Chalkboard and chalk; or large poster paper and markers; or overhead projector and blank transparencies
- Photocopies of the closing prayer for session 2 and discussion guide for session 3 for distribution to each group member

Opening

Introduce any newcomers and supply them with a copy of *The Active Life* and photocopied discussion guides. Invite participants to voice any lingering comments or questions from session 1.

Read aloud the poem by Chuang Tzu on pages 37 and 38 of *The Active Life.* Ask the group to share what images of modern society this poem suggests to them.

Reflecting Together

Begin the discussion of chapter 3, using the discussion guide questions. Don't feel that you must "get through" all the questions. Choose those you think are most valuable for discussion, or ask the group which questions they want to discuss. Remember to allow ten minutes at the end of your session for "Looking Ahead" and "Closing."

1. What do you think is the strongest criticism of "the active life" in Chuang Tzu's poem?

Answers will vary. Possibilities include: action for action's sake, without any understanding of the purpose behind it; action in order to prop up one's ego rather than to serve others; action to manipulate others in order to serve one's own ends.

2. In what areas of your life have you tended toward reaction rather than action—that is, living your life not from your sense of who you are and what you want to do, but from your "anxious reading" (p. 39) of how others define you and of what the world demands?

Answers may be very personal here and therefore difficult for some to share. Encourage those who feel free to describe their experiences to do so, or use Palmer's examples on page 40. Consider pairing off to discuss this question.

3. How does a "self-sustaining identity" (p. 40) free individuals for authentic action instead of reaction?

Possible answers include: a strong sense of self provides the security necessary to stand firm against external pressures to conform; self-awareness means we can live out our own dreams instead of other people's (p. 42).

4. What are some of the ways in which we live out others' dreams instead of our own? (See p. 42.)

Encourage participants to think in a variety of contexts: family expectations; our projection of what others expect of us; institutional demands, such as educational, religious, or governmental.

5. Do you agree with the author that professionals in our society especially tend to get caught in the "world of objects"

(p. 41) by creating dependencies on their professional techniques, and thus manipulating people instead of serving them? Why or why not?

A helpful vehicle for discussion here could be Palmer's example of the psychiatric facility as an illustration of the tendency of professionals to "create" clients (pp. 42–43). Ask participants whether they agree with the author's analysis of this incident.

6. What are some ways in which authentic action points beyond the one who acts to "that underlying reality, that hidden wholeness, on which we all can rely" (p. 44)?

Here it might be helpful to encourage participants to think about what authentic action looks like when applied to the contexts Palmer discusses, such as work done by professionals. Or, ask for responses based on the group's perceptions of their own opportunities for authentic action.

7. What does the concept of "hidden wholeness" mean to you?

Encourage a variety of responses. As a reference, see Palmer's introduction of the term on pages 29 through 31. He describes it as "the source and the power that make us fully alive" (p. 34).

8. One of the distortions of the "reactive life" is self-fulfilling prophecy (pp. 45–48). In your experience, what kinds of "false beliefs" have the power "to bring those falsehoods into being" (p. 45)?

Invite participants to share examples from their lives or the life of someone they know. Responses might include: low self-esteem can lead to failure; a sense of personal hopelessness can cause an individual to stagnate; the feeling that one person can't change things can lead to inaction.

9. Do you think the parable of the scorpion and the wise man (pp. 47–48) supports or contradicts the following statement?

"Ultimately good acts are those that allow people the freedom to choose their own destinies . . . [including] the other person's freedom to choose hell in a handbasket" (p. 47). Briefly explain your opinion.

Palmer thinks the parable contradicts this statement, because the wise man would have made a wiser choice to let the scorpion make its own decision, rather than forcing his "goodness" on it by rescuing it. In Palmer's interpretation, the scorpion was rejecting rescue by stinging the wise man repeatedly. Therefore, the wise man should have listened to what the scorpion was telling him and let it drown.

10. "Despite our pretensions, there are some things we simply cannot make. Why do some of us have such a hard time accepting that elemental and obvious fact?" (p. 50). How would you answer this question?

Invite participants to share their responses. For further discussion, encourage them to think about the difference between a healthy acceptance of our limits or our lack of control versus giving up in discouragement because we feel inadequate or powerless.

11. Palmer maintains that authentic action is based on the conviction that life's unearned gifts—the "raw material itself"—provide the foundation for our ability to act. Do you agree with this perspective? Why or why not?

Palmer explains that this sense of gift contrasts to our assumptions that we are totally self-sufficient and therefore "make" our own lives. Participants may have divergent opinions regarding what is given to us in life and what we create out of life.

12. According to Palmer, how are joy and despair dependent upon whether we are living in the shadow side of the active life or with a healthy understanding of authentic action? (See pp. 51–52.)

Use the definitions of despair and joy on page 51 to guide your discussion regarding the ultimate results of the shadow side of action versus authentic action.

13. "According to the new view of science, all of reality is active and interactive, a vast web of mutual relationships. . . . As knowers we both act and are acted upon" (p. 52). How might this understanding of reality affect our actions in the world?

Possible answers include: we will live with a sense of humility and concern for others in our actions; we will seek to care for and nurture what has been given to us rather than arrogantly exploit it.

Looking Ahead

Make sure all group members have a copy of the discussion questions for session 3. Ask them to answer these questions after reading chapter 4 of *The Active Life* before your next meeting. If they are keeping journals, ask them to consider sharing entries or thoughts from them when you begin the next session.

Closing

Distribute copies of the closing prayer for session 2. Read it out loud, either all together or as a litany:

> *Leader:* Lord, lead us into lives of authentic action,
> *Response:* not defensive postures of reaction.

> *Leader:* Open our eyes to the realities behind our acts:
> *Response:* the internal realities in our own heart and soul;
> the external realities of the world we live in;
> the transcendent reality of your immanent
> presence with us.

> *Leader:* Give us vision to see that we are all related

Response: in the great tapestry of your design.

Leader: Grant us courage and wisdom to weave our individual threads

Response: in gladness and confidence;

Leader: grant us humility and peace as we are woven together

Response: in the hidden wholeness of your Spirit.

Alternate closing: Stand in a circle and join hands as a way of symbolizing the relational reality that connects individual human beings. Invite participants to voice their hope for group members in the coming week. (For example, "My hope is that each of us has an opportunity in the coming week to experience a sense of life as gift.")

Session 3: The Nature of Right Action

The Active Life, chapter 4

Session Objectives

- To examine models (positive and negative) of right action in story form

- To explore the factors of motives, skills and gifts, "the other," and results that have a determining influence on the quality of right action

Session Materials

- Extra photocopies of the discussion guide for session 3

- A Bible for each participant, or for every two participants

- Chalkboard and chalk; or large poster paper and markers; or overhead projector and blank transparencies

- Photocopies of the discussion guide for session 4 for distribution to each group member

Opening

Invite participants to share entries or thoughts from their notebook or journal, if they have been keeping one during the course of this discussion group. To include others who haven't been keeping a journal, ask participants to reflect on their overall responses so far to Palmer, the book, or the subject matter.

Reflecting Together

You may want to begin by asking each participant to identify one or two questions he or she would most like to discuss.

1. **Do you recognize your own experiences anywhere in the Taoist stories of the woodcarver, the archer, and the butcher? If so, describe your experience(s).**

Invite group members to share their experiences, or to pick out themes or human tendencies they recognize in these stories.

2. **The woodcarver lists several distractions that he over-came in order to do his work: "trifles, that were not to the point"; "praise or criticism"; "my body with all its limbs"; "all thought of your Highness and of the court." In what ways do you think these distractions occur in our lives today, inhibiting our ability to perform creative work or authentic action? Describe those that are most significant for you.**

Individuals will have many different ways of interpreting how these distractions operate in their lives. For Palmer's examples of defenses that inhibit our freedom to work creatively, refer to pages 57 and 58.

3. **Using the stories of the woodcarver and the archer as examples to stimulate your thinking, describe what you feel are some ways to overcome the distractions you listed above.**

The way out of these distractions is by "fasting," "forgetting," and "dying." The woodcarver provides a positive example, the archer a negative example.

4. **The woodcarver's right action is described as "action that is harmonious with his own reality and with the reality around him" (p. 58). What does this definition mean to you?**

One way of understanding this concept of harmony is through Palmer's discussion of the "hidden wholeness" (p. 44) of things, which points to the nature of reality as "a vast web of mutual relationships" (p. 52).

5. **Why do you think the master surgeon advised her students that at one point in open-heart surgery, "You have only**

thirty seconds to tie off this artery—so you have got to take your time" (p. 62)?

A helpful reference here is Palmer's distinction on page 55 between right action and "the frenzy that we in the West often equate with active life."

6. "We often must launch our actions from motives and circumstances that are less than ideal," writes Palmer. "If we wait for the ideal motives before we act, most of us would never act" (p. 59). What life experiences have you had in which you started out with the wrong motives, or someone else's reasons, but ended up benefiting because you discovered your "own inward truth," or learned something in the process that transcended the limits of the original circumstances?

The woodcarver's process of finding his freedom (p. 60 and onward) is a primary example here, but Palmer's friend entering college (pp. 59–60) also provides an illustration of this process. This question lends itself to discussion in twos or threes, because the experiences may be difficult to share in a group setting.

7. The woodcarver walked "into and through" the fears that could have paralyzed him, and "found the freedom to act on the other side" (p. 60). What is most helpful to you in the process of getting through your own fears or prisons to claim your own "inner liberty"?

One answer is the woodcarver's fasting as an "active refusal to ingest, to internalize, the poisoned baits that can kill the spirit of right action" (p. 61). Other possible responses could include the support and counsel of friends; prayer, meditation, or other spiritual disciplines; personal disciplines such as writing, thinking, or physical workouts; plunging into the very thing that is most threatening.

8. Check your level of agreement or disagreement with the following two statements.

"Every human being is born with some sort of gift, an inclination or an instinct that can become a full-blown mastery. . . . Each of us is a master at something, and part of becoming fully alive is to discover and develop our birthright competence" (p. 66).

- ☐ Strongly agree
- ☐ Agree
- ☐ Unsure
- ☐ Disagree
- ☐ Strongly disagree

"Our tendency to identify ourselves with our acquired skills rather than our natural gifts is one of the less desirable habits of the ego. . . . Because the ego's identity is so heavily invested in these acquired skills, it does not want to acknowledge the natural, untrained, effortless gifts over which the ego has no ownership or control" (pp. 66–67).

- ☐ Strongly agree
- ☐ Agree
- ☐ Unsure
- ☐ Disagree
- ☐ Strongly disagree

Encourage participants to explain their reasoning behind their responses to these statements. Palmer refers to the findings of depth psychology (p. 68) in support of these statements.

9. To get in touch with your own version of the woodcarver's mastery, recall any activities from childhood that evoked your energies in a pleasurable, unself-conscious way. What kinds of experiences do you remember?

Share reminiscences freely. For further discussion, ask how many participants are continuing these activities in one form or another in adulthood.

10. The woodcarver and the butcher provide examples of sensitivity to "the other" in the process of right action. In your experience, what are some other examples of authentic action in which a "live encounter"—between "the inward truth of the actor and the inward truth of the other" (p. 71)—is an essential element?

As group members share their examples, ask them to explain why it is important to "know and revere the nature of the other" (p. 69) in order for action to be fruitful in those contexts.

11. Look again at the butcher's description of the "tough joints" (pp. 72–73) he encounters in his work. Think of one major context of action in your life, such as a significant relationship, a type of work, or a creative pursuit. Where are the tough joints for you in your relation to "the other," and how do you respond when you feel them coming?

The butcher's contemplative action in penetrating the truth of the other heightens his sensitivity and guides him in his responses. Share examples with one another from your own contexts.

12. "Perhaps the obsession with getting results deforms our action more than any other element of the active life" (pp. 73–74). Do you agree with this statement? Why or why not?

Encourage participants to share their reasoning about obsessive or healthy concern for results. Palmer lists several reasons why obsession with results deforms action: the image of the outcome supersedes the truth of what is happening; we close ourselves off to the opportunities in the unexpected; we focus on unrealistic criteria, such as "effectiveness."

13. The author speaks of the need for "confidence that life is trustworthy, that a life of live encounters will take us toward wholeness" in order to overcome preoccupation with results and transcend the need to predict or control outcomes (pp. 74–75). Do you feel deep down that life is trustworthy, and

that "live" encounters with others will lead toward wholeness?

☐   Yes, because . . .

☐   No, because . . .

Palmer encourages us toward this confidence because of his belief in the underlying unity and interconnectedness of all life.

Looking Ahead

Distribute copies of the discussion guide for session 4 to all participants. Ask them to read chapter 5 of *The Active Life* and answer the accompanying questions from the guide.

Closing

Ask volunteers to read aloud the following Scripture passages while the group prays silently or reflects on them:

Psalm 139:23–24
Mark 8:34–35
Luke 18:16–17
Philippians 3:12–14
Hebrews 12:1–3

Alternate closing: Read aloud "The Woodcarver" (pp. 55–56) or "Cutting Up an Ox" (pp. 72–73).

Session 4: The Lessons of Failure

The Active Life, chapter 5

Session Objectives

- To understand that the path to action leads to immersion in the reality of our relationship with others
- To explore the self-transforming nature of action, particularly in the process of learning compassion through suffering and failure

Session Materials

- Extra photocopies of the discussion guide for session 4
- A Bible
- Chalkboard and chalk; or large poster paper and markers; or overhead projector and blank transparencies
- Photocopies of the discussion guide for session 5 for distribution to each group member

Opening

As a way of reflecting back on the first three sessions, read aloud the closing paragraph of chapter 4 of *The Active Life* (p. 77). Share with each other what each of you feels you are crafting with the authentic action of your lives.

As usual, there are probably more questions listed in this session than you will have time to discuss. This chapter in particular may provoke intense discussion, especially over the issue of the nature of God. You may want to share with the group the "objectives" listed above as alternative ways to focus your time together, and then select questions according to what the group decides. Or, simply ask participants to circle the two questions they most want to discuss, and then select those that draw the most attention. This process may well refocus your objectives for this session.

Reflecting Together

1. Can you identify with the angel in Martin Buber's story ("The Angel and the World's Dominion," pp. 79–81) in any way? Why or why not?

As a reference for your discussion, consider Palmer's discussion of varying views on the angel, including his own, on pages 81 and 82.

2. If you were the angel in this story, would you have been satisfied with God's response at the end (p. 81)? Why or why not?

Questions about God raised by this story are pursued later in the chapter and this session (see questions 9–11, below).

3. When we experience failure, we can choose either "to allow the limits of life to diminish and embitter us, or to embrace those limits in ways that expand and illumine our lives" (p. 88). What do you think most influences which path we will choose?

See Palmer's discussion of false versus true understandings of reality on page 89.

4. What has been one of the most significant experiences of failure in your life, and how did you respond to it or grow through it? (Choose an experience from any time in your life, childhood or adulthood, in which you felt failure, regardless of whether by some standard you actually did or didn't fail.)

This question may be intensely personal for some people. Ask participants to pair off and share answers. Give them an out by suggesting that if the experience is too painful or personal to share, they could reflect in general terms about what they learned about themselves through it, without recounting specifics of the event.

5. **Do you agree that right action cannot occur from a distance, that it can only take place when we immerse ourselves in the reality of relationship with others? Why or why not?**

Palmer maintains that right action cannot occur from a distance because we will have no idea what the real needs are (p. 84).

6. **Why do you think people have a tendency to dispense advice in an attempt to "fix" someone else's struggle instead of providing simple companionship along the way?**

Palmer's example of his friends' varying responses to his own bouts with depression (p. 85) provides a helpful vehicle for discussion here. The angel's experiences are another way of approaching this question.

7. **Right action, according to Palmer, depends upon whether it is organic, or "true to the nature of things" (p. 86). How do you think we know when our action is based on the true nature of things, and when it is based on illusion?**

Encourage participants to share from their own experience. As a reference, see Palmer's analysis of the three elements that turn the angel from do-goodism to compassion (pp. 86–87). Palmer's key point here is how failure strips us of our illusions. The "learning cycle" of contemplation-and-action (p. 91) is also a helpful reference here.

8. **What do you think are the most important factors in whether success and failure contribute to our growth as persons or work against it?**

See the discussion of failure as key to our growth, on pages 87 through 89. Refer back to the angel's experiences of initial success and subsequent failure as another springboard for discussion.

9. **What do you think of the God in Buber's story?**

See the varying views presented on pages 90 through 94.

10. "If reality is a continual process of co-creation between ourselves and God, as I believe it is, then God is not a fixed quantity in some cosmic equation. Instead, God experiments, succeeds, fails, changes, learns, suffers, enjoys, and grows— just as we do" (p. 92). Check the phrase below that best characterizes your response to this statement.

☐ Strongly agree

☐ Agree

☐ Unsure

☐ Disagree

☐ Strongly disagree

Share with each other how and why you respond to this description of God, which is foundational to Palmer's approach in this chapter. The paragraphs from the bottom of page 96 through the middle of page 97 provide a fuller explanation of the statement above. To help focus the discussion for those with varying doctrinal convictions, consider raising this question: "Is God dependent on our action in the world because God *is not* all-powerful and all-knowing; or, is God dependent on our action in the world because even though God *is* all-powerful and all-knowing, God chooses to be vulnerable and not to exercise deterministic control by freely entering into partnership with human beings?"

11. What is your concept of the ultimate reality that is the context for our action—the "cosmic stuff" (p. 90) our lives are embedded in? (If it's helpful, frame your thoughts in terms of what you believe is the Great Work that human beings should be doing.)

Encourage participants to think about how their worldview, spiritual convictions, religious tradition, and so on, influence their approach to the meaning and purpose of human action.

12. "Suffering can never be solved. It can only be shared in compassion, shared in community, and every effort to put ourselves in charge of the relief effort weakens the very sharing in which our hope resides" (p. 97). How would a person's agreement or disagreement with this statement shape his or her view of right action?

A strong theme in the chapter is the ultimate goal of action, provoked by the angel's story—to live compassionately in community, or to try to fix problems from a distance. Palmer's experience with the white suburban church (p. 88) provides a helpful vehicle for discussion here.

13. What do you think are the most profound lessons that failure can teach us, when we are open to being transformed by it?

Palmer suggests that our most painful failures can save us from the illusion of self-sufficiency and open us to the centrality of relationship, to our need for community (p. 98).

Looking Ahead

Remind the group that the next session covers two chapters of *The Active Life*, not just one—both of which focus on episodes from the narrative accounts of Jesus' life. Suggest to the participants that they consider looking up these accounts in the Bible and reading the surrounding contexts to become more familiar with them, as time and inclination permit.

Distribute the discussion questions for session 5, pointing out that there are an extra number of them. Ask the participants to be thinking about which questions they want to discuss, since you won't have time to go through all of them (unless the group desires to take an extra session for them). Remind them to read chapters 6 and 7 of *The Active Life* and answer the discussion questions before session 5.

Closing

Ask a volunteer to read aloud Romans 8:28. Invite those who wish to do so to pray freely and spontaneously with short phrases of thanks to God for the lessons of failure. Close with your own brief prayer. (A suggested prayer: "Thank you, Lord, that failure need not have the final word in our lives. Use it to expand and illumine our lives rather than diminish and embitter us. Send us out into the world with a deeper understanding of our relationship to you, to our fellow human beings, and to all creation. Transform us according to your purposes in the Great Work of your Spirit.")

Alternate closing: Read aloud together the following quote from John Donne, and then spend a minute in quiet meditation on it: "No man is an island, entire of itself; every man is a piece of the continent, a part of the main; if a clod be washed away by the sea, Europe is the less, as well as if a promontory were, as well as if a manor of thy friends or of thine own were; any man's death diminishes me, because I am involved in mankind; and therefore never send to know for whom the bell tolls; it tolls for thee." (From *Devotions upon Emergent Occasions.*)

Session 5: Acting on the Truth

The Active Life, chapters 6 and 7

Session Objectives

- To explore how right action is based upon the truth by studying the example of Jesus

- To understand how temptation can lead us into the truth on which right action is based

- To consider how the illusion of scarcity and the truth of abundance are foundational assumptions shaping our action

Session Materials

- Extra photocopies of the discussion guide for session 5

- A Bible

- Chalkboard and chalk; or large poster paper and markers; or overhead projector and blank transparencies

- Photocopies of the discussion guide for session 6 for distribution to each group member

- A good dictionary

Opening

The two chapters covered in this session focus on events in the life of Jesus. Before you begin discussion on what you can learn from Jesus as a model of right action, spend some time sharing with each other your basic assumptions about Jesus himself. Throw open the question, "Who do you say Jesus is?" Ask participants to reflect on how their views align with or diverge from Palmer's treatment of him in these chapters.

Ask participants to voice their desires regarding which questions you will reflect on, especially since this session covers the material of two chapters and therefore includes a few more questions than in other sessions. Decide together what you will cover, and then begin your reflection time.

Reflecting Together

1. In what ways can temptation function as an initiation into the world of right action?

See Palmer's discussion of the function of temptation in Jesus' life, on page 101.

2. Where are the "deserts" in your life—the places in which you face the most difficult challenges in acting on the truth?

This question provides an opportunity for intimate sharing. Pair off in twos, each with a different partner than last session, to discuss your responses.

3. If temptation can either lead us into truth or deceive us into believing an illusion, should we seek temptation or shun it?

See the discussion on pages 103 through 105 about negative and positive views of temptation.

4. "The real work" of temptation is "to go where we are led, to see what is there, to respond out of our own truth" (p. 112). What does the phrase "our own truth" mean to you?

See Palmer's discussion of truth as personal rather than propositional (p. 112) as a reference here. This question is intended to help participants identify their understanding of what "the truth" is for them, as a basis for right action.

5. Why is it often difficult to act on the basis of our own inner truth and the truth around us?

Encourage the group to share from their own experience about the obstacles that get in the way of acting on the truth. There are many possibilities here: human nature, the unexamined life, sin, dysfunctional patterns learned in family life, the complexity of life's challenges, and so on.

6. **Think about your own struggles to act on the truth of who you really are, rather than on the pressures you feel to live up to an image (of your own making or someone else's). What help or encouragement can you find in how Jesus responded to the temptation to prove his identity?**

There are many possibilities here: Jesus was grounded in the truth of his own identity, and so when the moment of testing came he was able to rise above the pressure of external demands; Jesus responded out of his own definitions of identity, and rejected the definitions that others (for example, the "devil") created for him; Jesus acted according to his own inner truth, not according to a concern for visible results.

7. **"Right action is no more or less than the action it is right to take, taken without anxiety about results" (p. 115). What can Jesus teach us about letting go of an unhealthy concern for results?**

Palmer emphasizes Jesus' refusal—through struggle—to internalize other people's expectations for his life. Jesus' emphasis on doing the will of his Father is also relevant here, a faithfulness echoed in the remark of Palmer's friend in chapter 4, "I have never asked myself if I was being effective, but only if I was being faithful" (p. 76).

8. **"Right action demands that we find a deeper and truer source of energy and guidance than relevance, power, and spectacle can provide" (p. 119). What is this source for you?**

Encourage all answers, which may come out of a variety of religious, spiritual, and personal convictions.

9. **Palmer remarks that Jesus' desert encounter proves that he was "perfectly capable of resisting false action" (p. 123). Where do you think Jesus got the strength for such resistance, and where do we get it?**

Based on the emphasis in chapter 7, one source is the abundance of community. Other possibilities include God, a strong sense of self, and intimate relationships.

10. Do you agree with the author that scarcity is an illusion and abundance a reality? Why or why not?

Refer to the discussions on pages 124 and 125, regarding false assumptions of scarcity, and on page 128, regarding the transition to recognizing the potentials of abundance.

11. How do these fundamental assumptions about scarcity and abundance shape the nature of our action?

Palmer provides many contemporary examples on pages 125 and 126. He also contrasts Jesus' actions with those of his disciples based on their underlying assumptions regarding scarcity and abundance.

12. In your opinion, to what extent does community give rise to abundance?

The discussion of the feeding of the five thousand is intended to illustrate how abundance and community are inextricably linked.

13. In what ways do we overlook the gifts and resources immediately available to us—"those resources already present to us in the abundance of life itself" (p. 129)?

The emphasis in the chapter is on the ability to multiply material goods and inner well-being through sharing in community. Palmer's Chinese friend who created a meal and a community encounter (pp. 133–34) provides an example. "Our making is always a mixing of our ideas and energies with the abundant gifts of nature" (p. 129).

14. What is your concept of "abundance"?

See the discussion on page 132 regarding the meaning of Jesus' rebuff to the devil, "People do not live on bread alone."

15. Read the following statement, and then check your level of agreement with it. "At best, and at worst, the theology that makes Jesus a one-and-only incarnation of the Christ tends to excuse the rest of us from responding to human hungers with everyday actions that incarnate God's abundance" (p. 136).

☐   Strongly agree

☐   Agree

☐   Unsure

☐   Disagree

☐   Strongly disagree

Share your answers with each other. As a reference, see Palmer's discussion of incarnation on pages 135 and 136. This discussion can include not only doctrinal questions about the singularity of Jesus, but also how and what we are incarnations of in our action, and what it means to "incarnate the Christ-life." Have someone read aloud the definition of "incarnation" from a good dictionary.

16. Palmer's discussion of Jesus' feeding of the five thousand is centered on the significance of the miracle of community, inspired by the radical openness of a leader who trusted the reality of abundance in authentic community. What do you see as the lessons of greatest significance in this story?

Encourage group members to voice their own responses to the story. Perhaps in the enrichment of shared views, your group will create its own example of the abundance of community.

17. "Community and its abundance are always there, free gifts of grace that sustain our lives. The question is whether we will be able to perceive those gifts and receive them" (p. 138). What do you think is most important in developing awareness of and appreciation for these gifts?

The thrust of *The Active Life* points toward right action itself as a major way of revealing the true reality around us, as in the disciples' discovery that their actions led to the miracle of abundance. A helpful reference here is Palmer's emphasis on how a life of contemplation-and-action is the route to discovery of the hidden wholeness of reality—for example, see page 34.

Looking Ahead

Remind the group that session 6 is your final time together, unless you decide to extend the group's time to include an extra session for additional reflection on any issues that participants want to explore more fully. Distribute the discussion questions for session 6, and ask the group to read chapter 8 of *The Active Life*. Explain to them that there are many questions in the discussion guide for chapter 8 because of the weighty issues raised, so they may want to select only those questions that most interest them in the time they spend prior to this final session.

Closing

Ask a volunteer to read aloud Hebrews 4:14–16. Spend a minute in silent meditation on these verses, and then invite participants to voice brief prayers of thanks for: the example of Jesus; how God can use temptation to lead us to right action; the abundant gifts God has given us.

If the group would rather not engage in free prayer, close your meditative time on the Hebrews passage with this prayer (or one of your own):

> Lord, thank you for the faithfulness with which you lived your life and laid it down. We come before you in glad relief that you are intimately familiar with the human struggle to live in the truth. Open our eyes to see the truth through the illusions we are tempted to believe; open our hearts to embrace each other as sisters and brothers instead of strangers; open our hands to share our resources in the abundance of community.

Alternate closing: Spend a minute in silent meditation on this quote from Jesus: "The truth will set you free." Then take a few minutes to share with each other your thoughts—in brief, simple form—about how truth sets us free.

Session 6: The Horizon of the Active Life

The Active Life, chapter 8

Session Objectives

- To interact with Palmer's concepts of death, life, resurrection, and community
- To explore what each person believes to be the ultimate horizon toward which his or her life is moving

Session Materials

- Extra photocopies of the discussion guide for session 6
- A Bible for each participant, or for every two participants
- Chalkboard and chalk; or large poster paper and markers; or overhead projector and blank transparencies

Opening

Spend a few minutes discussing this statement and the question following it: "Every life is lived toward a horizon, a distant vision of what lies ahead" (p. 139). What is the horizon—death, new life, or other—that you feel you are moving toward? Then select the questions you wish to reflect on for this session, leaving fifteen or twenty minutes for closing. There are many questions included in this session because of the weighty issues Palmer explores.

Reflecting Together

1. How important do you feel ultimate questions (such as whether we are moving toward death or new life) are in shaping our approach to the active life?

Use Palmer's opening discussion (pp. 139–40) as a reference for this question as you share your responses.

2. Review the apocryphal tale about the apostle Peter on page 141. What does this story suggest to you about why we are tempted to cling to distortions of reality, physical handicaps, illnesses of the spirit, dysfunctional patterns of behavior, and so on?

Palmer explains that we perversely prefer the safe, comfortable, and predictable to the uncertainty and potential loss experience of change, new life, health.

3. The author mentions struggles with depression as his own experience of "favoring death over life" (p. 141). What experience(s) have you had in which you wanted to cling to an unhealthy, destructive, or death-embracing condition?

This may be too personal to share in a group setting. Suggest that participants pair off as they wish and share answers. Give them an out by suggesting that if the details of the experience are too private, they could share simply whether or not they wanted to cling to it—that is, "stay depressed"—and why.

4. In what sense is new life demanding and threatening?

Reasons mentioned on page 142 include loss of the familiar and the potential introduction of difficult demands or tasks. Much of chapter 8, in its treatment of Esquivel's poem, explores the concept of why resurrection is threatening.

5. What evidence do you see that our society—or human culture in general—is dominated by an attraction to death?

Examples on page 142 include violence-laden forms of entertainment, technological threats, the prevalence of war.

6. Where do you think lies the strongest hope for reversing the tendencies toward death or destruction in our society?

Answers may vary according to religious, political, and personal convictions. The primary emphasis in chapter 8 is on a universal concept of "the community of creation" in which we understand ourselves to be related to, sustained by, and responsible for the web of life that God has created.

7. What do you think are the effects when our society—or human culture in general—resists the inevitable by attempting to deny death?

One effect is that we become "lifeless," because we're pouring our energies into an illusion instead of embracing the reality of death and moving through it to the new life on the other side.

8. What kinds of impressions or responses do you have in reading Julia Esquivel's poem "They Have Threatened Us with Resurrection"?

Encourage participants to react to the poem itself. Refer to the background on pages 143 and 144 and the analysis on pages 146 through 149 only when it would provide a helpful clarification of specific elements in the poem.

9. Check your level of response to the idea that "all forces in life, those of death as well as of life, may work ultimately for good, whether they intend to or not" (p. 148).

☐   Strongly agree

☐   Agree

☐   Unsure

☐   Disagree

☐   Strongly disagree

Share your answers with each other. Ask participants to reflect on how their convictions about ultimate reality, or the horizon they are moving toward, shape their belief about whether circumstances ultimately work together for good. A biblical reference here is Romans 8:28, which you may have read aloud in your closing to session 4.

10. Palmer describes resurrection as a material affair, which transforms the material of the universe into different forms in cycles of change, death, and new material or new life. How does your concept of resurrection differ from or harmonize with this representation?

See pages 149 to 151 for Palmer's treatment of resurrection as material. To avoid getting off on tangents, guide the discussion toward how our concept of resurrection affects our approach to right action.

11. To what extent do you agree with the concept of nature's "holiness" (see p. 151)?

Share your responses. One way to approach this question is by considering the relation of God and nature—see pages 150 and 151.

12. Do you think we have to come to terms with death in order to experience life at its fullest? Why or why not?

Palmer suggests that we must "allow death to hollow us out"—that is, be willing to accept and experience the void it creates—in order to be "filled with life's presence" (p. 151). He returns to this on page 155, with the discussion of the illusion of denying death, and the truth of finding our lives only when we lose them.

13. Drawing on Esquivel's imagery, Palmer presents resurrection as giving birth to "an entire people arising as one and becoming a community in which injustice is no more" (p. 152). What is your response to this understanding of community?

Responses may range from the desire to become committed to such an effort to disbelief that such an entity is possible.

14. What do you think would be the greatest impact of "bone-deep knowledge of resurrection" (p. 153) on our action in the world?

According to Palmer, it would free us to risk everything, including our lives, in the effort to create a just community.

15. In what sense are the realities of community and individuality counterbalancing poles of a paradox?
See the discussion on page 156. A helpful reference here is the discussion in chapter 2 (p. 15) of the paradox of contemplation and action—one cannot exist without the other. You might also apply Palmer's concepts of separation, alternation, and integration (pp. 15–16) as stages of movement in working out the relationship of community and individuality in our lives.

16. The themes of death, life, resurrection, and community are woven together in the image of losing the life of the autonomous self and finding the life of the self embedded in community (p. 156). What other images of what we lose and what we find are suggested to you by the statement, "Only when we lose our lives will we find them" (p. 155)?
Encourage a variety of responses in order to mine the riches of this statement. Helpful references here are the biblical texts that give rise to it—Matthew 10:38–39, Mark 8:34–35, Luke 9:23–24 and 17:33, John 12:25. For each reference, ask one person to look it up and read it aloud, so all five can be read in rapid succession.

17. What areas of concern or giftedness seem to be the most fruitful contexts for you to live the active life?
Use this question to help participants think through the concerns, responsibilities, or contributions they feel called to—family growth, relationships, healing, empowerment, social action, reconciliation, peace, justice, artistic or creative pursuits, community relations, education, the world of ideas, spirituality, and a host of others are all possibilities. Another way to pose the same question is, "What do you feel to be your part in the Great Work?"

Closing

Spend some time sharing your responses to the question, "What have you experienced or become aware of in this study, or during our time together, that is likely to have the most significant influence on your life?" Invite participants to read from personal journals, if appropriate. Give the group a minute or two to gather their thoughts after you ask the question, before anyone responds.

Close your discussion by joining hands in a circle, and praying briefly for each other whatever you desire God to do in your lives as a result of this group study of *The Active Life*.

Alternate closing: Same as above, except instead of praying, voice to each other your wishes for the impact that your group study of *The Active Life* will have on your lives and relationships.

Materials for Group Distribution

Session 1: The Paradox in Becoming Fully Alive

Read *The Active Life,* chapter 1, "Spirituality in Action: On Being Fully Alive," and chapter 2, "Action and Contemplation: A Living Paradox."

1. What questions or reflections about your own life, if any, do Palmer's insights in these first two chapters stimulate for you? Briefly describe these questions or reflections—or why you don't have any yet.

2. The following pair of statements is one way of representing the opposing tensions of the active life and the contemplative life:

> "Don't just stand there—do something."
> "Don't just do something—stand there."

In your experience, how are these statements reflected in society—including religious communities—today?

3. Palmer defines action as "any way that we can co-create reality with other beings and with the Spirit" (p. 17). According to this definition, what are some of the ways in which you live the active life?

4. Palmer defines contemplation as "any way that we can unveil the illusions that masquerade as reality and reveal the reality behind the masks" (p. 17). According to this definition, what are some of the ways in which you live the contemplative life?

5. According to Palmer, we should "try to live responsively to both poles of the contemplative-active paradox. But we must honor the pole of our own calling, even as we stay open to the other, lest we lose our identity, our integrity, our well-being" (p. 7). As a help for understanding the journey of your own soul, use the following chart to identify your personal tendencies along the continuum between action and contemplation. For each set of poles, check the box along the continuum that best represents you.

	Strongly dominant	Tends to dominate	Blend	Tends to dominate	Strongly dominant	
Action	☐	☐	☐	☐	☐	Contemplation
Do	☐	☐	☐	☐	☐	Think
Spontaneity	☐	☐	☐	☐	☐	Preparation
Outward	☐	☐	☐	☐	☐	Inward
Struggle	☐	☐	☐	☐	☐	Quietness
Interaction	☐	☐	☐	☐	☐	Solitude
Take risks	☐	☐	☐	☐	☐	Plan ahead
Act	☐	☐	☐	☐	☐	Analyze

6. An "instrumental" act is one taken in order to reach some pre-determined end or result. An "expressive" act is one taken simply because it expresses one's inner gift or truth, without worry over "how things will turn out" (see pp. 23–24). What are some areas of your life in which an expressive understanding of action could encourage you to take risks by relieving anxiety over results or outcome?

7. Contemplation takes place in spontaneous moments of insight as well as in structured techniques—". . . life makes contempla-tives of all of us, whether we want to be contemplatives or not. The only question is whether we can name and claim those moments of opportunity for what they are" (p. 26). How would you advise an action-oriented person to recognize and learn from opportune moments of contemplation?

8. In the paradox of "contemplation-in-action," both tensions are necessary. "When we abandon the creative tension between the two,. . . action flies off into frenzy . . . contemplation flies off into es-capism" (p. 15). How can these opposing tensions work together to help us learn to "celebrate the gift of life"?

9. Palmer says that we have an inner voice that sometimes tells us,"We need to accept death . . . or we will spend our energies building houses of cards . . . [Death] will sweep all our works away " (p. 20). How do you respond to this voice? Do you agree with it? Why or why not?

10. What makes the difference between action that is fueled by an inflated ego and action that contributes to the development of a healthy ego?

11. "Contemplation and action are not high skills or specialties for the virtuoso few. They are the warp and weft of human life, the interwoven threads that form the fabric of who we are and who we are becoming" (pp. 18–19). How can these two dimensions help you grow into a stronger sense of self and a better understanding of your place in the world?

12. The author's mountain-climbing story (pp. 32–33) illustrates the active life as risk. Have you ever had an experience in which you knew you had to go all the way through it—"ride the monsters all the way down" (p. 33)—because it defied all your efforts to control or manage it? If so, what did you learn from the experience?

Session 2: The Shadow Side of Action

Read *The Active Life,* chapter 3, "'Active Life': The Shadow Side."

1. What do you think is the strongest criticism of "the active life" in Chuang Tzu's poem?

2. In what areas of your life have you tended toward reaction rather than action—that is, living your life not from your sense of who you are and what you want to do, but from your "anxious reading" (p. 39) of how others define you and of what the world demands?

3. How does a "self-sustaining identity" (p. 40) free individuals for authentic action instead of reaction?

4. What are some of the ways in which we live out others' dreams instead of our own? (See p. 42.)

5. Do you agree with the author that professionals in our society especially tend to get caught in the "world of objects" (p. 41) by creating dependencies on their professional techniques, and thus manipulating people instead of serving them? Why or why not?

6. What are some ways in which authentic action points beyond the one who acts to "that underlying reality, that hidden wholeness, on which we all can rely" (p. 44)?

7. What does the concept of "hidden wholeness" mean to you?

8. One of the distortions of the "reactive life" is self-fulfilling prophecy (pp. 45–48). In your experience, what kinds of "false beliefs" have the power "to bring those falsehoods into being" (p. 45)?

9. Do you think the parable of the scorpion and the wise man (pp. 47–48) supports or contradicts the following statement? "Ultimately good acts are those that allow people the freedom to choose their own destinies . . . [including] the other person's freedom to choose hell in a handbasket" (p. 47). Briefly explain your opinion.

10. "Despite our pretensions, there are some things we simply cannot make. Why do some of us have such a hard time accepting that elemental and obvious fact?" (p. 50). How would you answer this question?

11. Palmer maintains that authentic action is based on the conviction that life's unearned gifts—the "raw material itself"—provide the foundation for our ability to act. Do you agree with this perspective? Why or why not?

12. According to Palmer, how are joy and despair dependent upon whether we are living in the shadow side of the active life or with a healthy understanding of authentic action? (See pp. 51–52.)

13. "According to the new view [of science], all of reality is active and interactive, a vast web of mutual relationships. . . . As knowers we both act and are acted upon" (p. 52). How might this understanding of reality affect our actions in the world?

Closing Prayer for Session 2

Read the following prayer out loud, either all together or as a litany.

Leader: Lord, lead us into lives of authentic action,
Response: not defensive postures of reaction.

Leader: Open our eyes to the realities behind our acts:
Response: the internal realities in our own heart and soul; the external realities of the world we live in; the transcendent reality of your immanent presence with us.

Leader: Give us vision to see that we are all related
Response: in the great tapestry of your design.

Leader: Grant us courage and wisdom to weave our individual threads
Response: in gladness and confidence;

Leader: grant us humility and peace as we are woven together
Response: in the hidden wholeness of your Spirit.

Session 3: The Nature of Right Action

Read *The Active Life,* chapter 4, "'The Woodcarver': A Model for Right Action."

1. Do you recognize your own experiences anywhere in the Taoist stories of the woodcarver, the archer, and the butcher? If so, describe your experience(s).

2. The woodcarver lists several distractions that he overcame in order to do his work: "trifles, that were not to the point"; "praise or criticism"; "my body with all its limbs"; "all thought of your Highness and of the court." In what ways do you think these distractions occur in our lives today, inhibiting our ability to perform creative work or authentic action? Describe those that are most significant for you.

3. Using the stories of the woodcarver and the archer as examples to stimulate your thinking, describe what you feel are some ways to overcome the distractions you listed above.

4. The woodcarver's right action is described as "action that is harmonious with his own reality and with the reality around him" (p. 58). What does this definition mean to you?

5. Why do you think the master surgeon advised her students that at one point in open-heart surgery, "You have only thirty seconds to tie off this artery—so you have got to take your time" (p. 62)?

6. "We often must launch our actions from motives and circumstances that are less than ideal," writes Palmer. "If we wait for the ideal motives before we act, most of us would never act" (p. 59). What life experiences have you had in which you started out with the wrong motives, or someone else's reasons, but ended up benefiting because you discovered your "own inward truth," or learned something in the process that transcended the limits of the original circumstances?

7. The woodcarver walked "into and through" the fears that could have paralyzed him, and "found the freedom to act on the other side" (p. 60). What is most helpful to you in the process of getting

This discussion guide may be photocopied for local use.

through your own fears or prisons to claim your own "inner liberty"?

8. Check your level of agreement or disagreement with the following two statements.

"Every human being is born with some sort of gift, an inclination or an instinct that can become a full-blown mastery. . . . Each of us is a master at something, and part of becoming fully alive is to discover and develop our birthright competence" (p. 66).

☐ Strongly agree

☐ Agree

☐ Unsure

☐ Disagree

☐ Strongly disagree

"Our tendency to identify ourselves with our acquired skills rather than our natural gifts is one of the less desirable habits of the ego. . . . Because the ego's identity is so heavily invested in these acquired skills, it does not want to acknowledge the natural, untrained, effortless gifts over which the ego has no ownership or control" (pp. 66–67).

☐ Strongly agree

☐ Agree

☐ Unsure

☐ Disagree

☐ Strongly disagree

9. To get in touch with your own version of the woodcarver's mastery, recall any activities from childhood that evoked your energies in a pleasurable, unself-conscious way. What kinds of experiences do you remember?

10. The woodcarver and the butcher provide examples of sensitivity to "the other" in the process of right action. In your experience, what are some other examples of authentic action in which

a "live encounter"—between "the inward truth of the actor and the inward truth of the other" (p. 71)—is an essential element?

11. Look again at the butcher's description of the "tough joints" (pp. 72–73) he encounters in his work. Think of one major context of action in your life, such as a significant relationship, a type of work, or a creative pursuit. Where are the tough joints for you in your relation to "the other," and how do you respond when you feel them coming?

12. "Perhaps the obsession with getting results deforms our action more than any other element of the active life" (pp. 73–74). Do you agree with this statement? Why or why not?

13. The author speaks of the need for "confidence that life is trustworthy, that a life of live encounters will take us toward wholeness" in order to overcome preoccupation with results and transcend the need to predict or control outcomes (pp. 74–75). Do you feel deep down that life is trustworthy, and that "live" encounters with others will lead toward wholeness?

☐   Yes, because . . .

☐   No, because . . .

This discussion guide may be photocopied for local use.

Session 4: The Lessons of Failure

Read *The Active Life,* chapter 5, "'The Angel': Action, Failure, and Suffering."

1. Can you identify with the angel in Martin Buber's story ("The Angel and the World's Dominion," pp. 79–81) in any way? Why or why not?

2. If you were the angel in this story, would you have been satisfied with God's response at the end (p. 81)? Why or why not?

3. When we experience failure, we can choose either "to allow the limits of life to diminish and embitter us, or to embrace those limits in ways that expand and illumine our lives" (p. 88). What do you think most influences which path we will choose?

4. What has been one of the most significant experiences of failure in your life, and how did you respond to it or grow through it? (Choose an experience from any time in your life, childhood or adulthood, in which you *felt* failure, regardless of whether by some standard you actually did or didn't fail.)

5. Do you agree that right action cannot occur from a distance, that it can only take place when we immerse ourselves in the reality of relationship with others? Why or why not?

6. Why do you think people have a tendency to dispense advice in an attempt to "fix" someone else's struggle instead of providing simple companionship along the way?

7. Right action, according to Palmer, depends upon whether it is organic, or "true to the nature of things" (p. 86). How do you think we know when our action is based on the true nature of things, and when it is based on illusion?

8. What do you think are the most important factors in whether success and failure contribute to our growth as persons or work against it?

9. What do you think of the God in Buber's story?

10. "If reality is a continual process of co-creation between ourselves and God, as I believe it is, then God is not a fixed quantity in some cosmic equation. Instead, God experiments, succeeds, fails, changes, learns, suffers, enjoys, and grows—just as we do" (p. 92). Check the phrase below that best characterizes your response to this statement.

- ☐ Strongly agree
- ☐ Agree
- ☐ Unsure
- ☐ Disagree
- ☐ Strongly disagree

11. What is your concept of the ultimate reality that is the context for our action—the "cosmic stuff" (p. 90) our lives are embedded in? (If it's helpful, frame your thoughts in terms of what you believe is the Great Work that human beings should be doing.)

12. "Suffering can never be solved. It can only be shared in compassion, shared in community, and every effort to put ourselves in charge of the relief effort weakens the very sharing in which our hope resides" (p. 97). How would a person's agreement or disagreement with this statement shape his or her view of right action?

13. What do you think are the most profound lessons that failure can teach us, when we are open to being transformed by it?

Alternate Closing Reading for Session 4

"No man is an island, entire of itself; every man is a piece of the continent, a part of the main; if a clod be washed away by the sea, Europe is the less, as well as if a promontory were, as well as if a manor of thy friends or of thine own were; any man's death diminishes me, because I am involved in mankind; and therefore never send to know for whom the bell tolls; it tolls for thee." (John Donne, from *Devotions upon Emergent Occasions.*)

Session 5: Acting on the Truth

Read *The Active Life,* chapter 6, "'Jesus in the Desert': The Temptations of Action," and chapter 7, "'Loaves and Fishes': Acts of Scarcity or Abundance."

1. In what ways can temptation function as an initiation into the world of right action?

2. Where are the "deserts" in your life—the places in which you face the most difficult challenges in acting on the truth?

3. If temptation can either lead us into truth or deceive us into believing an illusion, should we seek temptation or shun it?

4. "The real work" of temptation is "to go where we are led, to see what is there, to respond out of our own truth" (p. 112). What does the phrase "our own truth" mean to you?

5. Why is it often difficult to act on the basis of our own inner truth and the truth around us?

6. Think about your own struggles to act on the truth of who you really are, rather than on the pressures you feel to live up to an image (of your own making or someone else's). What help or encouragement can you find in how Jesus responded to the temptation to prove his identity?

7. "Right action is no more or less than the action it is right to take, taken without anxiety about results" (p. 115). What can Jesus teach us about letting go of an unhealthy concern for results?

8. "Right action demands that we find a deeper and truer source of energy and guidance than relevance, power, and spectacle can provide" (p. 119). What is this source for you?

9. Palmer remarks that Jesus' desert encounter proves that he was "perfectly capable of resisting false action" (p. 123). Where do you think Jesus got the strength for such resistance, and where do we get it?

This discussion guide may be photocopied for local use.

10. Do you agree with the author that scarcity is an illusion and abundance a reality? Why or why not?

11. How do these fundamental assumptions about scarcity and abundance shape the nature of our action?

12. In your opinion, to what extent does community give rise to abundance?

13. In what ways do we overlook the gifts and resources immediately available to us—"those resources already present to us in the abundance of life itself" (p. 129)?

14. What is your concept of "abundance"?

15. Read the following statement, and then check your level of agreement with it. "At best, and at worst, the theology that makes Jesus a one-and-only incarnation of the Christ tends to excuse the rest of us from responding to human hungers with everyday actions that incarnate God's abundance" (p. 136).

  ☐ Strongly agree

  ☐ Agree

  ☐ Unsure

  ☐ Disagree

  ☐ Strongly disagree

16. Palmer's discussion of Jesus' feeding of the five thousand is centered on the significance of the miracle of community, inspired by the radical openness of a leader who trusted the reality of abundance in authentic community. What do *you* see as the lessons of greatest significance in this story?

17. "Community and its abundance are always there, free gifts of grace that sustain our lives. The question is whether we will be able to perceive those gifts and receive them" (p. 138). What do you think is most important in developing awareness of and appreciation for these gifts?

Session 6: The Horizon of the Active Life

Read *The Active Life,* chapter 8, "'Threatened with Resurrection': Acts of Death or New Life."

1. How important do you feel ultimate questions (such as whether we are moving toward death or new life) are in shaping our approach to the active life?

2. Review the apocryphal tale about the apostle Peter on page 141. What does this story suggest to you about why we are tempted to cling to distortions of reality, physical handicaps, illnesses of the spirit, dysfunctional patterns of behavior, and so on?

3. The author mentions struggles with depression as his own experience of "favoring death over life" (p. 141). What experience(s) have you had in which you wanted to cling to an unhealthy, destructive, or death-embracing condition?

4. In what sense is new life demanding and threatening?

5. What evidence do you see that our society—or human culture in general—is dominated by an attraction to death?

6. Where do you think lies the strongest hope for reversing the tendencies toward death or destruction in our society?

7. What do you think are the effects when our society—or human culture in general—resists the inevitable by attempting to deny death?

8. What kinds of impressions or responses do you have in reading Julia Esquivel's poem "They Have Threatened Us with Resurrection"?

9. Check your level of response to the idea that "all forces in life, those of death as well as of life, may work ultimately for good, whether they intend to or not" (p. 148).

☐ Strongly agree

☐ Agree

☐ Unsure

☐ Disagree

☐ Strongly disagree

10. Palmer describes resurrection as a material affair, which transforms the material of the universe into different forms in cycles of change, death, and new material or new life. How does your concept of resurrection differ from or harmonize with this representation?

11. To what extent do you agree with the concept of nature's "holiness" (see p. 151)?

12. Do you think we have to come to terms with death in order to experience life at its fullest? Why or why not?

13. Drawing on Esquivel's imagery, Palmer presents resurrection as giving birth to "an entire people arising as one and becoming a community in which injustice is no more" (p. 152). What is your response to this understanding of community?

14. What do you think would be the greatest impact of "bone-deep knowledge of resurrection" (p. 153) on our action in the world?

15. In what sense are the realities of community and individuality counterbalancing poles or a paradox?

16. The themes of death, life, resurrection, and community are woven together in the image of losing the life of the autonomous self and finding the life of the self embedded in community (p. 156). What other images of what we lose and what we find are suggested to you by the statement, "Only when we lose our lives will we find them" (p. 155)?

17. What areas of concern or giftedness seem to be the most fruitful contexts for you to live the active life?

Additional Resources for Leaders

Buechner, Frederick. *The Sacred Journey*. San Francisco: Harper & Row, 1982. Lyrical, meditative, autobiographical reflections on the importance of "listening to your life." Especially fruitful for modeling and stimulating the process of discovering the truth of our own inner reality.

Campolo, Tony. *Wake Up America! Answering God's Radical Call While Living in the Real World*. San Francisco: HarperCollins, 1991. A challenging call and practical guide to the active life, considered in terms of Christian grass-roots ministries to bring about change in the United States.

Ellul, Jacques. *The Presence of the Kingdom*. Colorado Springs: Helmers & Howard, 1989. This seminal work by the influential social analyst/theologian calls Christians to a radical lifestyle in community, in direct opposition to the death wishes and destructive myths of contemporary culture.

Foster, Richard J. *Celebration of Discipline: The Path to Spiritual Growth*. San Francisco: Harper & Row, 1978. A contemplative treatment of the Christian life, focusing on spiritual disciplines—inward, outward, and corporate—that transform our everyday life and relationships.

Nouwen, Henri. *The Way of the Heart*. San Francisco: Harper & Row, 1985. The wisdom of desert spirituality applied to contemplative living amid the frenzy of contemporary life. Emphasizes the strength of contemplation in giving us insights into ourselves, our relationship with God, and our solidarity with others.

Other Titles in
Harper's Leader's Guide Series

Addiction and Grace by Gerald G. May

Forgive and Forget by Lewis B. Smedes

Letters to Marc About Jesus by Henri J. M. Nouwen

When the Heart Waits by Sue Monk Kidd

Faith Under Fire by Daniel J. Simundson

A Tree Full of Angels by Macrina Wiederkehr

The Coming of the Cosmic Christ by Matthew Fox

The Kingdom Within by John A. Sanford

Finding God at Home by Ernest Boyer, Jr.

Wisdom Distilled from the Daily by Joan Chittister.

Life Together by Dietrich Bonhoeffer.

The Sacred Journey by Frederick Buechner.

Answering God by Eugene H. Peterson.

You can order any of Harper's Leader's Guide Series books through your local bookstore or by writing to Torch Publishing Group, HarperSan Francisco, 151 Union Street, Suite 401, San Francisco, CA 94111, or call us toll-free: 800–328–5125.